Love Shouldn't Hurt
Putting an End to Domestic Violence

Melissa Holmes

S.H.I.N.E. INC.

This book was sponsored through **S.H.I.N.E. Inc.'s**

Sponsor-A-Dream Program

For more information on having your dream of becoming an author sponsored email us at:

support@investinyouandshine.com

www.investinyouandshine.com

or call:

844-393-7446

ISBN: 1537689231
ISBN-13: 978-1537689234

FORWARD

Experiencing domestic violence is a reality some people live in on a day to day basis. Understanding the root of why this issue exists can be traced back to understanding the important components necessary for healthy relationships.

Creating a healthy relationship involves, having self-love first and foremost, practicing self-development habits on a consistent basis, engaging in effective communication, setting boundaries, and respecting the boundaries set by those you desire to build a relationship with. Respect in general is a huge component of building a healthy relationship. When you care about someone you show them respect, in fact respect is even higher than love on the list of important things to include in a relationship.

Respect acknowledges an individual's rights to free will as the infinite choice maker we all are. Love on the other hand says you care about a person so much you desire happiness for them unconditionally.

In contrast, domestic violence often occurs when someone has forgotten or refuses to adhere to the principles associated with respect. This can come out of fear of losing the person, being attached to the familiarity of the relationship, and perhaps even fear of being alone. Whatever the reason causing the behavior associated with domestic violence, whether it be physical, mental, or emotional abuse; there is no justification for the behavior.

In the Non-Fictional memoir 'Love Shouldn't Hurt' Melissa Holmes bravely shares the intricate details of what she experienced before she became an advocate for putting an end to domestic violence. Melissa shares her story in hopes of helping others to overcome the patterns of domestic violence.

If you'd like to learn more about her story, or need support as you take a step toward healing from abuse visit her website:

www.loveshouldnthurtny.com

TABLE OF CONTENTS

Forward

Table of Contents

Dedication

Acknowledgements

Legal Note

DEDICATION

This book is dedicated to my children Yasmin Figueroa and Darius Holmes, for never giving up on me when I wanted to give up on myself. They are why I fought so hard to survive. My mother who I love dearly words cannot express how much I love you mom.

ACKNOWLEDGMENTS

I'd like to acknowledge **April Diane of SHINE Inc.** for helping to make this book a reality and giving me the push I needed to become an author.

Tyron Whitaker who saved my life, and removed me from a bad situation.

Dr. and Deacon Williams – in Baltimore M.D, they counseled me while I was living in Baltimore. They took me under their wings and adopted me as their daughter. They prayed with me whenever I needed guidance. For that I am forever grateful, and love them to pieces.

Thank you to **everyone who has contributed to my success** thus far and to my readers for taking the time to listen to my story.

LEGAL NOTE

The views and opinions expressed in this text are directly related to the healing process endured by Melissa Holmes. As a way to heal she chose to seek counseling, therapy, and writing instead of taking any physical action by way of harm toward any human being. She took the time to educate herself and find the support she needed to take the proper course of action regarding the abuse she experienced. She in no way encourages illegal or life threatening behavior as a way to resolve domestic violence issues. She is an advocate for counseling and therapy. If you are in a situation like she encountered she recommends you seek help before things get out of hand. **The purpose of her sharing her story is to assist with putting an end to domestic violence**. Additionally, the views and opinions are not a reflection of the views and opinions of S..H.I.N.E. Inc. the sponsoring publisher.

1. I DIDN'T SEE SIGNS

It's a summer night in 1992, out celebrating my birthday with a few ladies, after dinner we ended up in a club, where I saw this 6'2 about 225lbs dark chocolate man, who later on I began to date. After dating for 5 years and 3 years after us having a son, he popped the big question of marriage. Being overjoyed I said YES. But nothing could have prepared me for years to come with this man who I thought I knew after five years.

After much consideration and talks, we finally had a date to get married, we had decided on March 21,1998. With the date set, it was time to put plans in motion for a wedding and to begin what I thought would be the happiest years of my life, which ultimately ended up with me spending the rest of my life with a man I later found out would turn out to be abuser. As the date approached things are wonderful and there was no reason for alarms to be raised.

The big day finally arrived. We had a small intimate wedding with about 80 close friends and family. It was such a beautiful day. With my son as my ring barrier at 2 years old and my daughter my flower girl at 10 years old, we were off to an amazing start. We continued our life as newlyweds on our honeymoon in the Bahamas where we enjoyed each other's company. stealing kisses and holding hands under the moonlight. Who would have thought this amazing being that I married would turn out to be the wolf in sheep's cloth

2. THE VEIL IS LIFTED

After being married at this point now for 2.5 years we were no longer in the honeymoon stage. With the honey moon stage long gone things start to get real. Now his true colors are starting to show, and no one even knows why. **So I think to myself something is wrong and I don't know what, the energy has definitely shifted** for the worse. There were a lot more unnecessary arguments for no reason at all. I thought to myself, "He can't be getting tired of my presence we work two different shifts." I worked from 9-5 and he worked the graveyard shift with lots of overtime. So now my curiosity is on high, wanting to know why the shift in his altitude has become more and more unbearable each day now. Now is when I'm starting to see anger and rage at things he had no control over.

One day we were both working and a fire broke out in the apartment across the hall. The fire caused our apartment to have water damage, the windows broken by the fire department and the front door was kicked in. When I received the call at work, I immediately called him to let him know what had happened. We both left work and arrived to our apartment at the same time, to find out it was much worse than anticipated, as we walked in the apartment everything was damaged, as we approached the living room he punched the bulb out of the ceiling fan and had shattered glass all over the floor. **Though very subtle** and possibly justifiable given the circumstances, this was another indication that **his way of dealing with life's challenges were irrational**.

I turned around to ask why would you do that, and he gave me this very cold look, so I asked why **he was angry at something we had no control over**. I never received an answer, but now the wheels in my head are turning, and I am totally confused. **That was the beginning** of me seeing a side I had never ever seen, this was all very new to me. So I suggested we have a talk about what happened, **he just wanted to move on after he apologized for his actions and assured me it wouldn't happened again**. It was the very first time, so I accepted his apology, a decision I realize in hindsight was me not **trusting my gut**.

Things began becoming more intense, he was becoming obsessive and very controlling, I asked myself, "what hell is happening right before my eyes?" Now he is calling me more frequently at work and during the night while he is at work. **I felt it deep in my soul** that something is most definitely wrong, but I couldn't put my finger on it just yet. The calls started to get more frequent over the next couple of months, and my anxiety started running on high. Every time I came home from work, **it was like walking on egg shells,** less talking but more arguing over petty stuff.

So I decided I was going to start going out on the weekends, since he was home he wouldn't mind watching the kids, while I got an outlet. So in the beginning he was fine with me going out with a girlfriend to the bar, where we would play pool, put money in the jukebox and laugh and drink. The bigger the arguments became during the week the later I would stay out on the weekend, because I couldn't take the arguing any more. I would cut the cell phone off to all calls when I was out and that just fuel him more. Turning my phone off was a way I used to attempt to get some peace of mind. Keeping my phone on felt like him intruding on my me time, he would call me at least 10 times throughout the night for stupid shit. I didn't want to deal with anything until I got home.

Now, I'm seeing a lot of rage from this man and it became crystal clear I didn't know the man I married, something had changed. So the air in the house started to get real thick, you could have cut it with a knife. This is the moment I realized I needed some space because he was beginning to smother me.

I mention to him how I was feeling. I felt like he needed to go to his mom's for a while and allow me some time to get my thoughts together. At that very moment I expected him to agree, because I figured he would not want things to get worse. I was so wrong in having those thoughts. His come back to what I had suggested was, "I am not leaving my home, my name is on the lease too and I don't have to leave." The moment that statement left his mouth I knew our marriage was headed for destruction. I just didn't know how fast it was going to happen. From that day forth **I saw him in a totally different light, my respect started to decrease** for the man I thought I would spend the rest of my life with.

3. THE WALLS OF SILENCE

Things began to take an interesting turn; we were no longer sleeping in the same room. I was sleeping in the bed; he was sleeping on the couch. The sex had completely stopped. He was doing his own laundry and cooking his own food. We had become roommates instead of husband and wife. I started hanging out more on the weekends without caring or feeling guilty. As a result, I could see his anger building up, but nothing could have prepared me for him striking me with a back hand slap that knocked me across the bed. This is where my nightmare begins.

At that moment when he struck me, I knew in my heart things would never be the same. He had crossed a line that there was no recovery from, he could apologize a thousand times, but he had already lost my heart from that one incident. Although I could accept his apologies, I would never forget how in that split second he had damaged my soul and my dignity. I knew I could not handle this type of treatment, but didn't know what I should do.

Too embarrassed to tell anyone because of judgement or criticism.

I decided to keep quiet and try and figure out, what I needed or could to do, all while praying that another episode wouldn't occur while trying to figure things out. I became very distant and cold towards him. I physically could not stand to be in his presence, so I started not coming straight home from work, because every time I knew I had to go home I would physically get sick. He tried to make things right but I was no longer interested in this marriage, he suggested we try counseling, I agreed but didn't give it 100%. After acknowledging counseling was not going to work, that just made things worse. He started to think I was seeing someone, but I wasn't. How could he not know his actions damaged our relationship? I thought to myself, "Is he fucking crazy or just plain stupid, does he really think we could ever have another chance at happiness." He must know he destroyed our family, so I refuse to feed his ego, because his ass was on borrowed time.

I realized the longer I stayed the worse things would get, it may even result in someone getting hurt or maybe even killed. I started having dreams at night, of killing this man. Dreams where I would be standing over this man with a butcher knife watching him as he slept, wishing he would wake up so I could cut his throat, because I wanted him to see it coming. That's when I knew something had to be done soon before this dream came true. I realized I was a ticking time bomb waiting to explode, he had pushed me to my limit in such a short time.

If you get to this point in your relationship, don't take it lightly. Thoughts are very powerful if left unchecked. These are clear signs your relationship has ended in your heart. Do yourself a favor, if the situation gets to this point and you are aware of volatile thoughts of this nature, make a plan of action to set you and the other person free, whether they are in agreement or not. No situation is worth you taking someone's life. Let God be the judge of destiny. Don't take a person's right to life into your own hands, take your right to make a quality of life choice for yourself and get out.

4. FOR BETTER OR WORSE

So it's the weekend again, and I'm going out to have a good time,
and this time I didn't plan on coming home until the sun came up.
When I arrived home, he was sitting in the living room waiting on
me. The minute I unlocked the door and pushed it open and saw
him sitting in the dark, I knew some shit was about to go down. I
was also praying this wouldn't be either one of our last days on
earth. I walked in and continued to the bedroom and pretended I
didn't see him, he followed me to the room, and stood in the
doorway of the room as I changed my clothes. He then started
yelling about the sun is coming up, saying "he hoped I had a good
time."

About 3 minutes into him yelling, I hear this loud thump and I
turned around to see what the noise was, and I saw him lying on
the floor. The first thing that came to my mind, God forgive me, is
"I hope he is dead." The noise had awakened the kids, they came
in my room and saw him on the floor. I was so disgusted and
angry, when my daughter said "mother call 911" I stepped over
him and preceded to the bathroom and I told her "if she wanted she

can call, cause I'm not."

When I came out the bathroom I stepped back over him to climb into my bed. He was foaming at the mouth and I didn't care. Soon after the ambulance arrived and asked questions, and wanted to know what happened, they said they were taking him to the hospital. I said, "alright," They said get dress we are going to need you to go with him, my thought "was for what?" I'm just coming in, I'm tired, so I suggested they call his mother in Queens, they insisted they would still need me because I was his wife.

Relationships require a level of commitment that for me at this point I was not freely willing to give. I felt this man was making my life a living hell, and now I had to show compassion and concern for someone I was not feeling compassionate or concerned about! Now I've been through some challenging things in my life, however; this unconditional love stuff in regard to this human being was one of the most difficult times of my life. I was being asked to show care for someone who clearly wasn't caring for my wellbeing. I felt violated and even more abused. However, in the moment none of this mattered. By law we were married, and that meant I WAS responsible FOR BETTER OR WORSE.

With this clearly being a model example of the worst, it was evident by looks on the police officer and ambulance professionals faces, that I needed to escort this man to the hospital, which I truly in my heart did not want to. When arrived to the hospital, he is immediately seen and given a complete blood work up. They wanted to determine if he had a seizure or not, he never had one before. The doctor pulls the curtains and walked in and said to us, they wanted to do a spinal tap to draw fluid to send to the lab.

I remember him being scared and me sitting in the chair by the bed with this stupid grin on my face. Now he needed me to hold his hand and all I could think of was walking out and telling him to kiss my ass as I exited the hospital. All the hell he was putting me through he had to be out of his mind. But I couldn't pass up the opportunity to see pain inflected on him, a part of me got pleasure out of it. When the doctors entered ready to do the procedure, and he reached his hand out for me to hold, I walked away and stood at foot of the bed. Within seconds he let out this scream from the needle entering his back, and I'm thinking good for you! Then he let out another piercing to the ear scream and I smirked. It is clear

to me as I stood watching this human being experiencing this

excruciating pain without an ounce feeling sympathetic that I am

completely detached from this man, this marriage, this part of my

life all together.

While, waiting for the results I'm looking at the clock ticking

away. After two hours of waiting the results were back, and there

were no signs of a seizure. They suggested maybe it was stressed.

Implying this may have caused him to fall out that morning. The

doctor asked what was he doing right be he fell, and I turned and

said with a grin "he was fussing with me because I had just arrived

home at 5:30 am from a night out." On that note the doctor, whom

I'm sure had seen his share of marital issues in his professional

career, proceeded to write his discharge papers and he was sent

home with a follow up appointment.

5. THE SAGA CONTINUES

In the back of my mind I thought this might have been a turning point for him. While our relationship was clearly over, I was secretly hoping that with the events that just occurred, my interactions with him would become more bearable. Which would make our inevitable divorce more amicable and at the very least tolerable. Again I was wrong.

As we approached labor day weekend of 2002, it's Monday and no work, but unfortunately I was home sick feeling very weak, running a fever and just real feeling irritated. I'm thinking it's going to be a quiet day, as I try and prepare to get the strength to go to work for the rest of the week. But things didn't happen that way, he started arguing I don't even know for what. I remember saying as sick as I am I going to try and make it up to 181st to get the kids some uniforms for school.

I got up to shower and prepare to leave the house. I get dress and headed out to the bus stop. About 10 mins after boarding the bus my phone rings, and it's him asking where am I. I said I'm on the bus I just told you where I was headed. When I had got off the

phone I really started to feel bad and felt like I couldn't make it

shopping. So I got off the bus and headed across the street to

Columbia Presbyterian Hospital emergency room, as I'm sitting in

the waiting area waiting for the triage nurse to call my name, I get

another call and it's him again, asking the same thing. "Where are

you?" I began to explain, "I said I got really sick on the bus and

couldn't make it to 181st, so I'm at the hospital."

He didn't believe me and came up to the hospital, I was dosing off

and when I opened my eyes he was standing over me. He startled

me, talking loud making a scene, people began looking at us. I get

up to walk towards the phone booths, he grabbed me up in my

chest, my feet were dangling as he yelled in my face, and called

me all kind of names. I was so embarrassed I couldn't go back in

the waiting area. When he put me down I ran to the ladies' room

crying in disbelief. I washed my face and pulled myself together,

he left for work out the front and I snuck out the back and jumped

in a cab.

This incident was the straw that broke the camel's back. I called my daughter while in the cab telling her I was on my way back, be ready we were leaving that night. I asked her where was her brother and she told me my husband had taken him to work with him. I made the decision to still leave with my daughter before he got back from work, and figured I would get my son the next day, but he had other plans.

Me on the other hand, I had only one plan. I had to get away, and at that point I would do so by any means necessary. Because I was feeling desperate I did not get to think things through. I was fearing for my life and the life of my children, I was out in the world alone with nowhere to stay with my daughter. If I thought that was the worse, it could get I was clearly wrong. He went to family court the next day and told them I abandoned my son, so he could get temporarily custody of him. A few days after he had his friend serve me with papers at my job, he had balls.

After being served with court papers at my job, I was fucking furious I couldn't believe this trifling ass man just did this I was devastated. Now I would have to take time off work to deal with this. So now I'm thinking messing with me is one thing but to bring innocent kids into this dysfunction has gone to another level.

As the court day approaches, I couldn't believe the man I married, was the same man I was experiencing now. As I sat and waited to be called into see the judge, my anxiety was on 1000.

Finally, our names are called and I'm so nervous because I'm not sure if I'm going to have my kids taken away from me or not. I felt like I was getting ready to have a nervous breakdown, I couldn't imagine being without my kids, I'm already alone, my marriage is dysfunctional, nobody knows what I'm going through. So we entered the courtroom, him on one side and me on the other, looking across the room with tears in my eyes, my soul was crushed, I couldn't pick my head up to look straight ahead because at the moment I knew I was BROKEN.

I couldn't believe things had gotten to this place in my marriage or life for that matter. I thought to myself, "what am I to do?" So now the bullshit begins, the judge starts asking him why he is there seeking custody, and he tells the judge he thinks he should get custody of my son, because I abandoned him and I have no place to live. He tells the judge I only took my daughter because I never wanted my son, hearing those words come out his mouth I totally

shocked me. It was clear I was sleeping with the fucking enemy for

years and didn't even know it.

I realized I was in the fight for my life, but had no clue how I was

going to survive. As the judge asked me questions, and I

responded, this cold feeling came over me. Then the moment I had

been dreading since I walked in that room came, the judge gives

his decision, he says to me, "when you come back to court you will

need to provide an address to where you are living, until then Mr.

Holmes will maintain temporarily custody of your son", I felt like I

wanted to die, I fell to my knees and cried like a baby. At the

moment I had no strength to stand to my feet, I was lost and alone,

and had to be escorted out of the room. I must have sat in the

waiting area for about an hour just crying so much I was making

myself sick, I started throwing up. He walked pass me and didn't

say anything to me. All I could think is how will I recover from

this, I wanted my son, I loved my son, and he strip me of him,

why? This was the man I loved, married, and had his only child, I

couldn't make sense of the non-sense that was going on.

I finally went in the bathroom and put some water on my face. eyes red and swelling all over my face. I now had to go get my daughter and go to hotel for the night and explain why I wouldn't be getting her brother. How do I tell her how I was betrayed by this man and he stole my son right out of my arms. now I'm thinking maybe that was his plan all the time.

As the night progressed, lying in that hotel room. I couldn't sleep. All I could think about was my son DJ and how I missed him so much. I just wanted to hold him and tell him I loved him and I was sorry. but I wouldn't get a chance to speak to him for about 2 weeks after the court date, I was hurting so bad I starting having cramping pains in my stomach that would last all day, I stopped eating regularly, I couldn't focus on anything not even work.

There is nothing in this world like a mother's love. Most mother will go to any length to protect their children. How do you, however; protect your child from someone who is supposed to love them just as much as you? I was beside myself with concern for the well-being of my son, however; I had to be strong for my daughter as well. I had to hold myself together so I could maintain the order of our lives so we'd have some hope of a brighter future

6. INSIDE JOB

The hardest thing I had to do was face the world, try and smile and be professional at work, when all I wanted to do was go into hiding, and pray this nightmare would end. Putting my head in the sand was not an option. I had faith and prayed often, but the nightmare would continue and just get worse over time. It was 3 weeks after our court date, and its lunchtime at my job and I'm covering the front desk for the receptionist. The front door opens and this guy walk in, someone I had never seen, he walks up to the desk and asked for me by name, then handed me this envelope and said you have been serve. He headed back towards the door, as I watched him walk out I proceeded to open this envelope, here I was hit with another blow, my husband served me at work with child support papers!

There were patients in the waiting area waiting to see the doctor, I couldn't leave and take a break, like I wanted to, for 15 minutes until the receptionist return. I felt like time had stopped and everything was moving in slow motion like I was dreaming or something, I wanted to wake up out of this madness, it was obvious he was trying to back me into a corner, and DESTROY

me any way possible.

By the next court day, I found out, he was getting inside

information, these things he was doing are things woman would do

to men. He could not be thinking of these things on his own, come

to find out he had starting dating a woman at the court house name

Marie, who had access to all my information, and was giving him

ammunition towards me, she was basically telling this man how to

DESTROY me. So far their plan was working. He had called ACS

and the court ordered me to do drug testing (urine and hair), I

missed my son's birthday and Christmas and so much more.

How do I explain to the child I gave birth to that he was being

brainwashed by his father? I knew I couldn't deal with this man

with my mind being clouded with emotions, I knew I had to be

100% mentally, he was, using everything he could to make sure I

never recovered from this heartbreaking trauma. By this time, I had

no more tears, I needed to figure out how to give this man a good

fight, and pick my head up and put on my boxing gloves and wax

that ass. Now that he had me backed into a corner, I knew I must come out fighting. I also knew I needed help to keep my mind balanced. I made an appointment to see my primary doctor, who then referred me to counselling, and the counselor ended up putting me on medication, that would help me deal with the difficult times.

After about 2 weeks on the medication I was sleeping better and was able to think a little bit clearer, I knew what I had to do. First I would comply with all court order request. By this time ACS was making unexpected visits to my daughter's school to make sure she was there daily. I was ordered random drug test, and I yet to figure out why. Until I reflected back on our early years of courting. I was able to put somethings together and had a breakthrough as to why I was being ordered for drug testing. Somethings I had shared with my husband in confidentiality when we were dating, about how I tried marijuana and coke years before we started dating was surely the reason these random drug tests were popping up.

Drugs weren't for me and I never used again, however, he went and told the courts I was getting high, and that's why I was ordered for random testing. I felt like I had been punched in the stomach.

Something I told him in confidentiality he used against me in court and was destroying my world of sanity. I would pass all the urine test and that wasn't good enough for him. So he asked them to take my hair, because he knew if they took my hair, I might fail because drugs stay in your hair. They can tell everything from how long you been using, and he knew they would take my kids from me including my daughter which wasn't his. Little did he know I wasn't using drugs. That was the moment those thoughts started again. I remember thinking "the only way out of this nightmare was to have him killed."

The actualization of these thoughts I was now having were totally out of my character, but I felt like I was left no choice. I was not going to have my kids taken away from me. I would kill him before I let that happen. I had taken the steps, I set us free in the hopes that we could move on with our lives. Why was he still trying to make my life miserable? It couldn't be because he loved me and wanted to be with me. This wasn't love! LOVE SHOULDN'T HURT! I just couldn't stop thinking this wasn't fair. He was the one abusing me, yet I was being punished.

With each day passing that thought of having him killed became stronger and stronger in my head, I could no longer fight the hatred I had gained for this man. I had become familiar with a man who was a bus driver, whose bus I would ride every day after work, he invited me out for drinks one weekend, and my friend and I went to this after hour spot to meet the bus driver on 5th avenue. By this time, we were dating for about 6 months and he was 52 years old when we met, I was 36 years.

I was upfront and honest about my husband, in my heart and mind it was over. As we became closer he introduced me to some of his biker friends at a biker party. One Saturday night we were out, and as we sat in his Jeep, I brought up what I was thinking, and he mentioned if I was serious he could connect me to someone. I couldn't believe his response, yet in my desperation, without hesitation I said, "I'm ready."

A few days later he called me with a meeting date and time, I was there with bells on. As I'm sitting in the Jeep with his connection talking, he asked about my husband's work schedule and a picture, he proposed to have him come up missing and never found. At the time, it sounded like music to my ears. I would be free to live a normal life again. Then I started thinking how I would be able to face my son every day knowing I had his father killed, could I really do it? My heart kicked in and I immediately started thinking more rationally as the idea of this being a reality become more possible. I'm no killer, how would I live with the guilt.

The fact that I was even thinking of this again and actually considering caring out plans to have him killed, brought tears to my eyes and full awareness how scared I had become and how desperate I was feeling to get my life back. In this moment I tell the connect I'd get back to him in a few days, and he agreed. My conscious saved his life that night. And so as the story goes he got to live a few more days making my life and lives of my children miserable. Until something gives.

7. THERE HAS TO BE A BETTER WAY

So what is a girl to do now, I needed to develop a clear plan of action of how I was going to regain my power and peace of mind in my life. I was in survival mode by all means necessary. I didn't make sense to me, how another woman, this Marie character, could help destroy another woman. A part of me wanted to confront the both of them, and give them a piece of my mind. After a lot of consideration, I realized confronting them was not a great idea, because I was extremely emotional and was not confident I could keep my emotions in check.

So now I had to think of something else more effective, and put my feelings on the back burning momentarily so I could come up with a powerful plan. A plan that would allow me and my children to regain peace in our lives. If I didn't think of something fast I was going to lose my kids, and possibly commit suicide if that happened. So my next thought was to seek professional guidance to see if they could assist with my dilemma.

With every passing day of not be able to see my son, I became more depressed with suicidal thoughts and even at times the recurring thought of killing him. I desperately yearned to find a common ground with this man, but that never looked like it was going to be in my future. He continued to taunt me every day about going to jail or being without my kids, how they would grow up to hate me because of things I did to him.

Upon all this pressure he was already causing in my life, he decided to add another blow with his threats of killing me. Now I'm realizing we were having the same thoughts but for different reasons. Mine was to be FREE of the abuse and his was because I wouldn't come back to him, and he wanted to be vindictive. So he began to tell me how he should kill me, but he would get his hands dirty so he would have someone else do it for him. I started living my life in fear from that point on, because I never knew if it was going to be my last day. I remember saying to him if you're going to do that I don't want to see it coming, have them catch me coming out from work, all I ask is you don't have me killed in front of my kids. By this time, he had worn me out physically and mentally, I felt like I had no more fight left in me, I was so tired.

I remember being on edge every day after the threats started. I felt like I was being held hostage in my own body. I was trapped and couldn't get out, all I wanted was peace of mind. This experience was physically making me ill. The dilemma was starting to show in my face and body. I looked tired every day, never getting my proper sleep or proper well balances meals. All the worrying was starting to take a big toll. I felt like I was having a meltdown, always crying, nervous, just a ticking time bomb waiting to explode, I needed to do something, but I realized I couldn't check myself into the hospital because he will have more ammunition against me. I decided to take a few days off from work to regroup, because at that point I had decided I was going to continue to fight until my last breath.

After taking 3 days off, nothing could have prepared me for what was going to happen on that 4th day, my life would take a turn for some sunshine. I arrived to work like every other day around noon my work phone rings and the person on the other ends says, "can I speak to Mrs. Holmes?" I asked, "may I ask whose calling" it was the nurse from Queens Hospital calling to tell me, my husband was found on the side of the road pulled over, turning blue. She continued to inform me he had stopped on the side of the road because he couldn't breathe, as she continued to bring me up to speed with the events of my husband's encounter a part of me wanted to hang up the phone, because I did not care what this lady said I was NOT going up to that hospital again and did not care what she said. She proceeded to let me know that by the ambulance got to him, he was having a really bad asthma attack, so I asked, "what did she want me to do" I'm sure she was taken aback by my very evident nonchalant attitude. I wasn't concerned, she did not know the story. She said he was in ICU, I told her to call his mother and hung up the phone. I know everyone knows what I'm thinking right now...

As I hung the telephone up, all I could think was I hope he dies. I couldn't believe I had allowed this man to take me this far out of my character and to the point where I would want to see harm come to anyone. Later that day, I received a call from another nurse saying that he was asking for me. He needed me to bring some items to the hospital. I laughed and told them it wasn't going to happen and they should call the bitch that's helping him try and destroy my life. Come to find out she did go to the hospital pretending to be his wife to gain entrance to see him.

However, she didn't know although I wasn't going to show up to visit, she wasn't either. While I couldn't bring myself to kill him, I was determined to bring some discomfort to him like he had done to me, so I put a restriction on his visitors. He spent 3 days in ICU with NO visits from me or anyone else. He remained in the hospital 2 more days after being moved to a regular room. When the day came for him to be discharged, He couldn't drive from Queens to Manhattan, he needed an escort home and to be taken care of while on leave from work for a few days. So my mother in law ended up going to get him and let him stay with her in Queensbridge Houses until he felt better.

8. A BLESSING IN DISGUISE

We had two more weeks left before we went back to court. I had to prove I had a stable place, although I had found a place in the Bronx, I decided not to give the court my information because of his inside connection. So because I didn't give them the information about my residence he kept temporary custody of my son. But that would be short lived, because he would not live to make it to our next court date.

May 5th of 2003, started out good, no complaints so far. Lunchtime was approaching and the office phone rang. Guess who it is? He threatened to come down to my job and make a scene. I couldn't talk to him on the phone, there was a waiting room full of patients waiting to see the doctor. "I cannot talk now" I inform him, and I hang up. He kept calling back to back being annoying, and I keep hanging up. The last thing he said before I hung up the last time, was "today your number is up." He had shaken me to the core. So as it got close to 5 o'clock, I decided to write a letter and seal it and put it in my desk.

I called my coworker on the phone and asked her to come to my desk, when she arrived I showed her the sealed envelope and asked her to give this to the police if I didn't make it to work tomorrow. She agreed she would. It was something about his voice this time that made me feel I was going to die that evening.

As I'm walking out of my office door all I could do was pray, as I'm walking to the train, my eyes are filled with tears and my heart in disbelief as to what I was up against. I was horrified at the fact that I would never see my kids or the rest of my family. I felt like I had been raped without physically being touched. My heart was bleeding as I couldn't understand how things had gotten this out of control.

Finally, I'm standing on the platform of the 4 train at 86th waiting to go uptown to get my daughter, and then head home to my new 3-bedroom apartment, that I had just started to decorate. I felt like I was not going to get a chance to enjoy my new home with my kids, even though he was not with me at the moment I knew in my heart I was going to continue to fight for my son and both my kids and I would be a family again that was my dream. I had started decorating my sons room and everything for when that time came.

Now I wasn't so sure about the possibility being a reality for us. I arrive to my destination to pick up my daughter and go home to Kingsbridge. Everything seems to being moving in slow motion. A part of me wants to savor the moment with my daughter and a part of me wants to rush home to safety. I decided we would stop and eat dinner at BBQS on Fordham, we get a table, order our food at least we were in a public place. Then BOOM, I remember the moment like a scene out of a movie. I get a phone call. The call I have been waiting for, for a long time that would change our lives forever.

My phone rang and it was the hospital AGAIN. This time the nurse on the other ended insisted I come down to see about my husband, because she informed me, that he might not make it. I arrive at the hospital with my daughter on my heals. Secretly praying this night mare was finally coming to an end. When I arrive I realize I may need to call in to work for tomorrow, as I could tell this was going to be a long night. After making a call to my jobs emergency number, I go back into the room to wait for the doctor, about 20 seconds he came in to say my husband expired.

Not shocked or surprise, my next question was can I see him one last time, everyone else was crying. The doctor says "we have to move the body to another room, then you can go in one at a time." While we waiting I go to call my mother-in-law to tell her that her only son and her baby boy had expired. This was the only time I felt something. My heart went out to the mother in her. I then went go back to waiting area waiting to see him, with anticipation I needed to see him to know this was actually real. The time has come to face the man who was making my life a living hell.

The doctor finally comes in to escort my daughter and sister who went in first, while my mother and I waited for their return. After about 3 minutes they return and my daughter is crying hysterically, so now it was my time and I was so ready for this. The doctor escorted us to the room but didn't go in with us, my mom stayed close to the door, and I walked right up to his body lying there still warm, with no shirt on and this tube sticking out his mouth and tape wrapped around his head. I got real close in his face to make sure he was dead and not breathing. I had no more tears once I realize I was free. One tear trickled down my face, as a sigh of relief. I felt like a ton of bricks had been lifted off my chest. I preceded to pat him on his chest and repeated these words, "I never wanted it to go down like this, but you have just given me two things back, my life and my son, and I could not have asked for much more" I patted his chest and left the room. My only regret was now I had to go back to my mom's to tell my son his father had just died. But honestly I was happier than a pig in shit. I was ready to make some calls and start giving out lap dances.

When we arrive back at my mom's to tell my son his father had died, I realized I was not prepared for this conversation as happy as I was, I wasn't happy to deliver this message to my son. After all this was still his father we were talking about. After giving him the news I say to him, "you will spend the rest of the week at grandmas to finish up the week of school," and I will be back here Friday to pick you up and take you home. It felt so good to finally be able to say those words to my son.

I had never ever forgotten about him. He already had his own room in the new apartment that his sister and I had started decorating way before his father's death came about. His room was decked out with Spiderman everything, sheets, comforter, curtains, brand new bed and a closet full of toys and clothes just waiting for his arrival. Friday was finally here and I was excited to pick him up from school. All I could do was smile and hug him so tight, I never thought this day would come after that last conversation with his father.

I was finally taking my son home, and I had never been more excited. Although I knew there was more struggles ahead of me with my son: from all the negativity his father has planted in his head, and the love he had for him. I had to now be patient with our growth together from this point on. It wouldn't be easy but I was ready for this one challenge.

Now it was time to make arrangements to put this asshole to rest. The to do list was long, making calls to his job and so much more, but the one I was really struggling with was going to the funeral home to pick out caskets, cause honestly speaking I wanted the cheapest shit they had. I didn't care how cheap it looked or anything. I even thought about having him cremated and just be done with it. But although I was in my feelings I couldn't do that because of my son, so I took the high road and did things the appropriate way. I decided to bury him in the same custom made suit we got married in, I sent him home in the same suit, shoes the whole nine.

After taking care all funeral arrangements, his mother agreeing to have him buried in a space next to his father, which was reserved for her. The time had finally come for everyone to say their goodbyes! The viewing day was upon us, people were showing up crying and flowers were being delivered. I had already given direct instructions to staff to screen all flowers that arrived with tags. Not to my surprise, guess who ordered some beautiful flowers with such a loving message, that was stopped at the door? Absolutely his mistress, Marie, who had become my worst nightmare.

I was called to the door, and the delivery person was ordered to take the flowers back to the flower shop or deliver to the person who ordered the flowers. To my surprise as I'm standing there with the delivery guy, who had balls to walk across the street with her sister, yes her again. Of course I'm supposed to be on my best behavior, but of course I was nice nasty with malice in my heart, and I stopped them both in their tracks and told them they were not welcomed and to please take their flowers and leave.

After standing there for some time demanding that she be let into the funeral home, and her realizing I wasn't going to change my mind, she decided to leave peacefully but not without mumbling a few words under her breathe. I think she realized at the moment her ship had sunk, and her plan to destroy me had failed. I so desperately wanted to put hands on her, but I realized I had the upper hand at that moment, and the tables had turned and her world was crushed. The man she claimed to love, although he was still married, and at some point thought she would have a future with was gone. Ha-ha, who got the last laugh, silly trick, tricks are for kids!! For a second I wished her heart would hurt like mine had been hurting for months before. I was in a dark place that would take time to heal. I took a deep breath in and thank God things were turning around.

Things were now coming to a closure or at least I thought so anyway. It was now time to go to the burial site. As my family loaded into the limousine to follow the body to upstate New York, to finally lay the soul to rest that tried months before to have the tables reversed, all I could think about was my mother could of been burying me, instead of his family burying him. We finally arrive to the spot right next to his father, who was also an abuser, and here they both going to lay next to each other. Both dead from cardiac arrest. His father died at 31 years old and my husband died at 33 years old. Two men who brought so much pain, are now back together once again to raise hell in HELL. As I stand there listening to people say such kind words about this young soul who died to young, in my head all I could think is "what the hell happened to this person they speak of," where did he go? Because I no longer knew him and didn't want to be at the cemetery anymore, I desperately wanted to scream hurry the hell up so we can head back to the city, I was ready to start my new profound life.

.

9. CASE CLOSED

It was finally over. I survived this ordeal and now it's time to repair

what had been broken. Like my credibility, and now I had to fight

hard to clear my name. We already had a court date coming up,

and he wasn't here. I got a chance to show up to this court date

with his death certificate in my hand. As I waited patiently in the

waiting area, the same area I sat in a few months before crying my

eyes out, while no one cared, now I was back with confidence,

head up and this huge smirk on my face.

I waited as they called our name, but this time ONLY one of us

would be entering the court room and I couldn't wait. Then the

sound I had been waiting for 'Mr. & Mrs. Holmes' came. The

court office called, and then I stood and he asked if the other party

was present. I said with this big grin 'he won't be making it," he

asked, "why" I took out the death certificate and said, "cause he's

dead." Lord you could never imagine how good that felt. He told

me to follow him in, I walked in confident I was about to be set

free again. The court officer explained to the judge the

circumstances. The judge then proceeded to bang the gavel and said ALL CHARGES DISMISSED. ALL child support, temporary custody, boom just like that. I was screaming once I left. The nightmare was over. It was finally over I could now breathe easy, knowing things would get better over time.

Then I was dealt one final blow. Marie would continue to send ACS information about me, to keep an open case on me. Two women showed up at my house 9pm one night, stating they had gotten information that my son was being neglected. That he didn't have food and no clothes or bed to sleep on. She also told them I used drugs. Now I'm mad as hell about all these false allegations against me AGAIN! I never felt so validated, they walked through my house, opened my cabinets, checked my kids room to make sure they had beds, and the most humiliating part was they ordered me to go take a drug test with a bunch of criminals, like I was on probation. I had to go to this beat up center, with a worker who watched me pee in a cup. I was out for blood, this must stop. I refused to continue this torture from her. Not from this day forward.

Now it was time to take off my gloves and stand up and reclaim my dignity, and prove to everyone, how my husband and his

mistress was out to destroy me and defame my character all to save

their own. I lived for the day to come face to face with this chick,

and I knew that time was coming real soon. So I kept telling

myself just be patient, cause every dog will have its day. So every

time I was ordered to have testing done, or there was home visits

schedule, I complied and rose to the occasion. This chick kept

allegations going on for 6 months after my husband died. Then

finally a worker showed up for what would be the last visit. They

didn't even conduct a full interview that day and immediately said,

case close. We can see this is some bullshit, so be expecting

paperwork stating case was unfounded. I was now completely free

to now live my life with my kids, and put all the tragedy stuff that

happen to us behind us, and move forward.

10. THE PERFECT GENTLEMAN

Moving forward it was 3 yrs. since my husband died in 2003.

Everything was going wonderful. I had a new job, the kids were

doing great and together again. I had been on vacation to Hawaii

with my husband's insurance money, I was in blissful heaven. Until I

hired a moving company to help me move in my new apartment little

did I know this was the beginning of the most horrific experience I

had ever had to encounter, worse than my marriage. I met my second

abuser, who worked for the moving company I hired. This

experience almost claimed my life.

It's been said **we repeat lessons until we heal and learn the lesson.**

I thought I was healed, and I definitely thought I learned my lesson

about being a better judge of character in regard to men. It had been

three years since my husband transitioned to the afterlife. I was

enjoying life and back to living free. Why on earth I attracted the

second abuser into my life remains to me a mystery.

It was moving day April 2006, the moving company sends me three guys to pack and move my stuff for me to my new apartment on Southern Blvd, in the Bronx across from the Bronx Zoo. Everything was going as planned, things were running smoothly. I thought one of the movers was very attractive, as I stood back and watched them do their thing. Finally, after about 5-6 hours I paid them and signed their paperwork and they left. The kids and I started to unload some of the boxes. Later that evening my cell rings, and it was the cute guy that moved me, telling me to check my microwave for my microwave plate inside to see if I had it, because there was one left in the truck. To my surprise the microwave plate was mine. He offered to drop it off to me the next day after he got off from work.

The next day he did just that and brought a nice bottle of wine along too. I thanked him for going out of his way to bring my item. I offered him a glass of wine and we sat and talked for about 2 hours. When it was time for him to leave, he asked if we could go out for dinner sometime. I said, "sure." It had been 3 years, I was feeling good. I thought I was ready to get back on the dating scene.

I will **never forget the events leading up** to us being an item. We made plans to go out. On our very first date he showed up with flowers (birds of paradise) to be exact, a perfect gentleman. He opened and closed doors, great conversation, really laid back well-kept individual, with a sense of humor; he could make me laugh. We had a nice dinner, just talking and getting to know one another. I Shared some of my past history of domestic violence with him, expressing how I could never ever go through that again. I let him know how that experience ripped me of my dignity.

After seeing each other for about 5 months, we decided to make it official, we were now a couple, but this fairytale was short lived after a year and a half. No one could of warned me for what mask destruction my life was headed for with a narcissistic abuser I will call Dee.

Now what really got me was when we first met, he introduced himself as Dee, and I was a little turned off because the man I had buried 3 years before, I use to call him Dee. I got this feeling about this name because I of the previous bad experiences with my husband. I tried to remain open minded and tried not to judge

because every individual is different. I decided to let my guard
down and give it a try only to be disappointed and **wishing I had
listen to my gut feeling** when he introduced himself.

After a year and half, something happened that will change my life
forever. To my surprise I became pregnant, and suffered a
miscarriage when I was 8 weeks along. There were no warning
signs I was aware of, it happened suddenly. By the time we reached
the hospital, I was in disbelief as to what had happened. Once we
arrived, I was ordered to have a sonogram, and we discovered the
baby was gone. There was no heartbeat. At that moment three
heartbeats were lost. The man who I thought would be there to help
me with this tragic loss was not going to be there for me at all. I
would later realize his soul died that day in the emergency room
along with my baby. For a month or so we tried to comfort each
other, but something had changed. I started to feel like I was alone
and very scared. It was really hard dealing with this miscarriage. I
started to disconnect and he started to show his true colors. The
more I cried the more he would yell, not trying to understand my
depression and stress. One thing was perfectly clear we were

dealing with this loss in different ways. I became depressed and he started to drink more after work. He went from drinking a 6 pack of Heineken, to two 6packs and a long neck. I realized I may have stepped right back in dog shit.

Although I was feeling a little uneasy about somethings, I had to try and get myself back on track. But he was making that difficult he started showing more and more anger, in the way he talked. He was also becoming aggressive with me. I couldn't understand the change, because I suffered the same loss. Then it became obvious that he blamed me for the miscarriage. Somehow he thought it was something I had done to cause the loss of my child. He hadn't actually said it yet, however; I could feel the energy of blame.

So a few days had past, and he began arguing about something small, and threw a plate up against the wall. At that moment I knew I was in another situation and it could possibly get worse. That same evening, he decided to get pissy drunk and hit me for no apparent reason, I was totally shocked and caught off guard. As I started to cry, he told me to shut the fuck up cause my tears did not faze him. I remember crying myself to sleep that night. Saying no not again, I wasn't mentally capable of dealing with this. I thought I would be on the verge of a nervous breakdown.

I started to feel on edge all the time, and very confused about what was happening in this relationship. I was aware that something was definitely wrong, things had shifted but I couldn't pen point why? So I said to him one night, we need to sit down and you need to talk to me about what's going on with you. The sad thing is, when we first made it official I had shared some of my darkest secrets about what had happened with my husband. He sat across from me at dinner that evening and said to me, you will never have to worry about that with me, because I would leave you first before I would ever have to put my hands on you.

So as we are talking I'm recalling that conversation and I brought that conversation to his attention, and he had this look of coldness on his face. After that night of reminding him of what he said, and what he had actually done, there was another shift in his demeanor. I felt like now I was walking on egg shells in my own home once again, he stayed angry all the time, I'm constantly telling this man how much I loved him, I did the cooking, the cleaning, washing clothes, you name it I did it.

I was reminiscing on how when I first moved in this apartment he helped me unpack boxes, he even took me grocery shopping the very first time, and loaded my refrigerator and cabinets. I so desperately wanted that man back, but he didn't know how to cope with the loss of the baby, and he wouldn't talk. All he wanted was to drown his sorrows and make my life miserable, and he would succeed in doing this for 4 years until the light shined my way.

But before the light would shine my way, I was accused of dealing with a handicap gentleman in a wheelchair who lived in the neighborhood. I would pay the ultimate price for just being friendly and saying hello. I can remember it was July 20th of 2006, because it was the day before my birthday, I went to the store to get a gallon of water. He had warned me many times before not to speak to the guy in the wheelchair, because he thought he was flirting with me, but I didn't think so. There were times I had continued to speak when he wasn't around, because I had felt like he had never done anything but speak and hold the door for me at the store.

So this day, I was coming out of the store with the water, and the guy in the wheelchair was coming in the store, but he held the door for me to come out. I turned to say thank you and then he preceded to say hello. So I said, "how are you." Not knowing Dee had come downstairs wondering what was taking me so long at the store. As I turned the corner I realize he was there, we walked half way in the block and he hit in my face and I flew into a parked car, the bag with the water went flying across the street. The street was full of people on this hot summer day, and no one helped me.

He simply walked away, then someone walked over to me asking if I was alright. I ended up calling the police, and someone else called the ambulance. Of course he had disappeared by the time police showed up, so I was loaded in the back of the ambulance, with an ice pack to my face, off to St Barnabas Hospital I went. It wasn't until arriving there did I know my nose was fractured, the doctor informed me after x-rays.

Now what happens next was totally new to me. doctors started asking a lot of questions, even the police showed up to inform me that they didn't catch him, and that they had gone to my house and he wasn't there. So at that point I was advised not to go back home that night, I should go to a friend or family member house. How could I do that, I'm thinking because I didn't call anyone while I was here to let them know what had happened. Then my phone rings and it's my friend Robin, who lives not too far from me or the hospital, so I pick up. She asks what I'm doing and with hesitation in my voice, I say I'm at the hospital and she gets frantic and says I'm on my way.

I didn't want her to come to see me like this, I was embarrassed and had been humiliated in the street. Before I could say anything else she had hung up, and a few minutes later I saw her walking into the emergency room. Robin was a firecracker known for stabbing men and women, immediately when I saw her I started crying all over again, as she hugged me and asked me what happened. She had asked me if Dee had done this and I held my head down in disbelief, she was pissed, and wanted to know where he was. I said I don't know, and she demanded that I go home with her. I was shaken because I didn't want to bring drama to her home she had two kids, but she stayed there until I was discharged just comforting me.

Robin had experienced similar abuse in her past and it had totally changed her and she began being aggressive and determined not to allow that to happen again. So she began being real vicious, her personality had changed totally. It's after 2 am on my birthday, and was being discharged from the hospital with a prescription for pain medicine and a follow up appointment for my nose. As I'm waiting for discharge papers I got this real uneasy feeling in my stomach, like something was going to happen when we left the hospital. I told her how I was feeling, and she assured me know worries and showed me a knife she had brought out the house. "Oh my God!" Were my thoughts because I don't want anything to happen to her especially for trying to defend me. All I could think about were my kids who were at my mom's for the weekend.

As Robin and I are leaving the hospital, we are talking and walking to her place not far away. As we entered to cross a side street, something drew my attention down the side street. I noticed a double parked car with two guys sitting on the back trunk facing the hospital. I immediately recognized one with a baseball cap on, even though they were a distance away I knew that man, and he recognized me too. As I alerted Robin that he was down the street, I peeped them jumping in the car to head us off around the block, before we could get to Robin's house. We continued to walk calm or at least I was trying anyway. We made it to Robin's house and as soon as she had the key in the door, this car came rolling up really fast, she opened the door and told me to go in and she closed the door, with her outside the door arguing with him, it was DEE.

Her son heard the noise and dashed out to see what was going on, as Dee was trying to push himself inside to get to me. He was yelling at the top of his lungs, calling my name, screaming I better come out. Finally, the police were called and he fled again before they arrived.

Now I'm really in my feelings about bringing this drama to Robins house who has kids. She fixed up the couch for me and I was so uneasy about being there I couldn't fall asleep after showering. I sat up in the dark just staring out the window, thinking about everything that had happened, and how my face was looking for my birthday July 21st. I also couldn't stop thinking about how embarrassed and uncomfortable I will now feel in the neighborhood. Each and every day I will now have to find the strength to face these people, who witnessed this man hit me and not come to my side. I had mix emotions, I was angry at myself, and I was angry at all that saw this crime happened and didn't assist. Finally, I drifted off and awoke in extreme face pain, I took one look in the mirror and was horrified at what I saw. Why? Why? Was this happening to me, what did I do to deserve this? I had no answers, at that moment I decided I wanted to leave New York. I didn't have any idea as to where I wanted to go but knew I wanted to go, I wanted to escape this nightmare.

11. THE GREAT ESCAPE

I started questioning myself, wondering if it was anything I was doing wrong, I couldn't understand how I could end up in two abusive relationships back to back. I was so confused, and needed answers, but had no idea how to get what I needed. I couldn't think clearly, but I knew I had to become a chameleon and camouflage myself. I started to have suicidal thoughts, he had broken me after hitting me in the street. At that moment I realized I was lost, I had never had suicidal thoughts even when I was at my worse with my husband. For the first time I really couldn't see the light at the end of the tunnel. This was the beginning of me falling into deep depression, in a black hole, sinking in quick sand real fast.

After returning home, 3 weeks after my birthday I made the decision to leave NY and move to Baltimore. Although I had no family there. I was leaving all my family back in NY. My mom was concerned about me leaving. By this time, I still hadn't said anything to anyone about me being abused.

My decision was made so now all was left was to execute my plan. So I started to look for places in Baltimore online. I came across a beautiful townhouse, 3 bedrooms, 2 full bathrooms, a basement

with washer and dryer, and a backyard. I reached out to the owner,

we spoke, and the woman was willing to work with me. So I made

arrangements to go down there; the day president Obama was

being sworn in because he had won the presidency. I remember

because there were no rooms available because everyone was

going out there to witness history. The owner was nice enough to

let me and my kids and mom who went with me to see the house

stay with her. I was excited for what I thought would be a new

start, but I was taught a very valuable lesson about trying to cut

cost on moving. Although I was ready to move for a fresh start, I

really didn't have the funds to hire a professional moving company.

So foolish me made a deal with the devil. **I was not thinking**

clearly.

The deal was, since Dee worked for a moving company, I would

rent a U-Haul truck and he would drive it down, set me up in my

house and leave and come back to New York. But after two days

the devil decided he wanted to stay. I was angry and upset because

we had a verbal agreement. Once down there, things had started to feel different, but my feelings for him was never going to be the same, because I would never forget the things he had done to me before. After moving to Baltimore, things were good for a while, then I just didn't want to be in his presence. As he tried to seek employment out there, I decided to keep my sanity that I would volunteer at my son's middle school. Because I was clinically pronounced disable a few years after my husband died and I had been hit by a car. So I felt the need to stay busy and occupy my time, so I could be relieved of some of the stress from home. The constant yelling, degrading and now alcohol was a part of his everyday life. When he wasn't drinking, he was stressing about the lack of hours he would work, everything became an issue.

Once again I started spending more time outside of home, but this time being productive at the school. I started to feel good about myself just a little and started doing my hair and stuff and caring about my appearance once again. I started to feel wanted and important, doing things that at one time didn't exist especially for a long while anyway. I felt different until it was time to go home, then my attitude would change, because I knew what awaited for me there. I could never let the people at the school know, because I would be back in the same shit I left in New York, they would take my son. So every morning I walked out the door to volunteer I would where this mask to cover my pain and all the dysfunction in my home.

This time I had totally lost myself, I no longer knew who that person was when I looked in the mirror. I started to get angry with myself, because I knew I deserve better, but I had started to come to the realization that maybe I was afraid to be alone. Although I still felt that a part of me knew this man was hurt by so many women. I thought if I could show him Melissa was different from every other woman that came before me, he could see how much I loved him, and would treat me different. That I loved him for him, but he couldn't see my faithfulness because he was broken. As the daily arguing became a routine at home, my feelings were changing for him. I even told him he was pushing me away from him. So I started making plans to go home to New York at least twice a month to visit my mom and daughter. My son and I would leave him for the weekend, and he started to accuse me of dating someone back at home in New York. Although I wasn't, I started

saying I was when he asked, because I got tired of being accused,

and explaining my whereabouts when I came to visit my family. I

actually started not to care, he was pushing me to that point of no

return.

12. TURNING THE TABLES

I remember saying to him, now it's starting to become crystal clear as to why every woman before me cheated on you. He was totally offended by that statement, he became irrational and couldn't believe I was saying such things to him. He started to tell me I was disrespectful, and I should talk less and listen more, and I laughed in his face. Because if he didn't know by now he was about to find out how feisty and ruthless my mouth was. I started to study him, to see what would push his buttons because I knew he was playing on those things he knew would set me off. I noticed he couldn't take my mouth, I was too swift and quick and he couldn't stand that. So he would say fuck you and I would say no fuck you and your drunk ass good for nothing mama. I would see how upset and confused he would get and I would continue to fire off like a machine gun until the gun was empty.

Now I knew what his weakness was and I continued to play on his weakness. Now things were starting to get really interesting, because he couldn't figure me out anymore. As I was volunteering at my son's school I started to inquire about therapy. I knew I couldn't exactly share with the school, in fear once again that they would report my situation, and I would lose my son to the Baltimore City System. So I became really close with the guidance counselor whom I started working closely with. She had referred me to this amazing therapist who was black and made house calls. Her first initial intake was done at my place of residence, with Dee upstairs trying to ear hustle, on what was taking place downstairs. She could tell something was extremely wrong.

I tried to remain calm as she grew more suspicious of my surroundings. The more she talked to me, the more, I started to feel extremely comfortable, in a way I had never felt with any other before her. So the day after I remember her showing up at my son's school, and asking to speak to me privately. I remember her saying to me how she too was abused years ago before she had decided to become a doctor. At that moment I felt like someone could actually felt my pain. During all our sessions after that day, I started to open up little by little and share my history all the way up until the day we met. The more I saw her the more the arguments became intense, because we started to meet away from my home and he could no longer listen or watch my every move. He couldn't figure out what I was saying and he wanted to know. I would lie and tell him something else, and he would hit me and try and blackmail me.

He becomes more curious with every passing day; he is now making it very easy to become something I'm not. With every day that went by I was starting to hate him more and more. I was now starting to see red, which is a sign I saw with my husband. Now I'm thinking this abuse is more brutal and may not have a happy ending for one of us. This is a feeling that is all so familiar to me, and hopefully I can figure this out before it claims a life, and I'm praying hard it won't be mine.

The holidays were approaching as I was preparing to come to New York with my son to spend with family until after New Year's. I would leave Dee in my home in Baltimore, so I decided this time I was leaving I wasn't paying any cable and buying any grocery. He would have to figure things out for himself. The cable, included no phone or internet service. I remember him calling asking me to call the cable to see what happened but I never did. I knew what to expect when I got home if he would have figured out that I hadn't paid the bill, but I had already started preparing myself to leave him. I started leaving important papers, clothes and others in New York with my mom.

While I was preparing to break away from this monster, things had taken a horrible wrong turn. I was enjoying a nice quiet evening at home, when he arrived home from work, things started out peaceful and we were being very civilized to one another. Then I realized he had brought a six pack of Heineken and placed them in the freezer. After his shower, and starting on his 4 beer of the pack, shit hit the fan really quick. He starting fussing and repeating the same stuff over and over again. I said to him please go lay down, I really didn't want to hear his mouth, and walked away and I headed to the bathroom. I reached the bathroom and locked the door, and pulled the toilet down to sit and just gather my thoughts. Now he is standing and yelling through the door, wanting me to open the door. I'm telling him I am not opening the door, because I knew what was next if I did. In a split second he entered the bathroom only for me to realize his intentions was to kill me when he entered.

13. THE WALLS CAME TUMBLING DOWN

Upon him entering the bathroom, there was fear that he would kill me. There was this look in his eyes I had never seen before, almost like someone else was standing before me. He approached me with this wild look in his eyes as I'm sitting on the toilet. Then there was silence as he grabbed my throat and starting choking me. I looked in his face, and tried to fight back as he applied pressure to my wind pipe. Tears rolled down my face, as he looked down in my face, I hear these words come out of his mouth, I could kill you right here and right now and sit here in the house with your body until your son comes home from school so I could see the expression on his face when he finds your body. It was crystal clear at that moment he was capable off killing me. As I started to lose conscious he let go within 10 seconds of me going out.

As he let my throat go I was totally uneasy and at that point very scared. I walked out of the bathroom after crying for about 15 minutes, and put water on my face to gather my thoughts on my next move. I walked to my bedroom only to pass him sitting in the living room watching t.v. like he didn't just tried to kill me moments earlier. As I walked passed him he said to me if you think about leaving I will kill your kids and your mom. I immediately felt sick on my stomach with fear that he would make good on what he said. All I could do was cry because I knew my back was up against a wall. I had no clue what to do. I knew I could never leave knowing he would do such horrific things all because of me. I was furious and all I could think is I wanted him dead by all means necessary. I knew right then I was in the fight of a lifetime for myself and my family once again. So I jumped into survival mode, and watched my every move very carefully.

Now is when I had to plan my escape. Although he had threatened my family I knew I would be stepping on eggshells as long as I was in the home. So I started to investigate, and realize there was a warrant for his arrest in New York because of child support. So as I would make trips to visit, I started leaving my important papers, and started going to the police department asking questions because I was in another state. I wanted to know if they would run his name through the system to see if it would show he was in Baltimore. Then I found out that his kid's mom would have to report his whereabouts, but that wouldn't do anything because he wasn't in New York. Now I would have to think of another plan to get away. Him getting locked up on a warrant would be a blessing that would happen. So with careful consideration I would think of a plan B, that would almost cause both of our families' great pain.

As I continue to brainstorm, I'm sitting up one night on my laptop, and I'm on Facebook just messing around, I had this ah ha moment that I wasn't going to renew the lease for my townhouse and was moving back to New York. The problem was I don't drive so I saw a friend on fb and said I need your help like yesterday, and he told me to call him the next day. Before I could get a chance to make that call things got out of hand really quick. The next day approached and I had a doctor's appointment. Upon arriving back home after the appointment, this funny feeling came over me. I felt like something was about to happen. I had never felt this feeling before, it totally scared me. But for a while, things in the house were quiet until Dee had a few Heineken beers, then he started tripping about something petty like dinner.

As he continues to yell at me from behind, I could see him

standing there once I looked up in my glass cabinets. I mumbled

something and he asked what did I say, and I told him I wish he

would go take a nap or something. I could see him moving behind

me. I quickly turned around and grabbed the knife I had just

cleaned off of the sink, and I put it up close to me by my breast, in

hopes that he would see the knife and not charge at me. But he

proceeded to attack me saying he will knock the shit out of me

again. He went to grab me and landed on the knife, as I was yelling

NO MORE, you are not going to hit me anymore. It happened so

fast, I was in the state of shock, I let go of the knife and ran out of

my home, running and screaming down the streets of Baltimore for

someone to help me because I thought he was behind me. I

managed to make it up to John Hopkins hospital and hid in the

ladies' room calling my son at his after school program, telling him

he had to leave now and meet me. He called when he arrived

outside and we caught a cab to the bus station and got on the last

bus which was 8 pm headed back to New York.

We made it in time to catch the last bus, upon arriving to the

station, I had to figure out what I was going to tell my mom. I had to call her and tell her that we were coming to New York. I knew

she would ask questions, and at that moment I didn't have any

answers for her. Things happened so quickly I didn't know if he

was still alive, or if he had made it outside to get help, all I knew

was I needed to save myself. This man had threatened my life one

time too many, my thought was it was now or never. The abuse

had gone on way to long, and I couldn't handle it anymore.

Once arriving I knew there would be plenty of questions to answer,

and I really didn't have any answers to give. So my mind was

racing as now it seemed as though we are safe, but I couldn't be

totally sure. How and why did this happened for the second time,

now I'm feeling like it's time for self-evaluation. By this time, I

was totally confused but knew I needed to stay focused on

surviving just in case he ever figured out where I was. Things

would now become more intense being back in New York at my

mom's. She wasn't in any predicament to help me, she was getting

older and more fragile, so things would get very complicated if my

abuser showed up here to harass or stalk me.

I thought I needed to put in place an order of protection and include every one that was in the house, but as I considered that idea, I had known that he had no respect for authority, so he would easily violate that order. Right as I thought things would begin to get easier because I had left, it didn't once he realized I was back in New York. Once he figured out I was at my mom's the calls started all day long, all times of night. He even went as far as to get other women to call and ask for me, or pretend to work for UPS. The women would act as if they had a package to deliver, or they would ask if I could meet the driver outside of the driver's route. It became clear after a while he was trying to get me away from my comfort zone to kill me.

After avoiding the calls and threats, I decided to report to the police department, how he was trying to kill me. Since I didn't have an address to where he might be staying in New York, there was nothing they could do. I would actually have to wait for him to try and kill me or kill me. By this time, I was feeling the stress I had brought back to New York. I was feeling like I should leave my mother's and go into a shelter. I figured this way she would be safe from any harm coming to her door. As long as I and my son were there the house was in danger. I remember he called one day 40 times, and I felt so bad. I went outside to walk around in the cold just crying, because for the first time I couldn't think of how to keep my family safe from a monster. I must have stayed outside for about two hours, my mom worried that he may have come onto her block. He was extremely smart not to come onto a block that I had grown up on, because he knew he would never make it out alive.

The calls continued which everyone upset my mom more and more. She started to worry that this man was not going to stop until he killed me. I hated that she was having these thoughts about her baby girl, the last child she bore. I couldn't understand why he would continue to taunt me and my family, I figured we weren't together that should of been the end of it. So I decided the next time a call came in I would accept it, and see what was going to be said. As I waiting patiently, finally the phone rings and it was Dee and not a female, he desperately wanted me to meet him on 125th and 8th avenue at 8 pm that evening. I knew if I went there was a good chance I would be killed. So I told him I was coming but didn't show up, but I went to speak to an investigator at the 30th pct., who suggested that if he called back tell him to meet you at the address of the pct., then you come here and wait for him to show up.

Soon after he did exactly what I thought and that was to call back to harass me. So I did exactly what the investigator suggested. I gave him the address to the pct. To my surprise when I went down to the pct. to wait for his arrival so he could be arrested once he entered the pct. I sat there for 2 hours and he never showed or called me back. So I figured maybe he had drove around and saw the address and at some point figured out what was going on, and left and never returned. After realizing he wasn't going to show up the officer escorted me back to my mom's home a block away to assure my safety. I was preparing myself for the annoying threatening calls but nothing. So I started to ask around to find someone who would go down to Baltimore with me to help me retrieve my furniture and things.

14. TAKING MY POWER BACK

Finally, I ran into a man I had dated when I was 16 years, as we talked, he asked what I had been up too. I confided in him what I was going through. He offered to help me with getting my belongings back to New York, I was relieved and truly grateful. So we set a date that we would rent a U-Haul truck and go to Baltimore to retrieve my things. When that day approached all I could do was pray that things would go smoothly, without incident. I didn't want any confrontation, or this man who is doing a good deed for me to get hurt on my watch. I could never live knowing that he got hurt protecting me. I remember crying most of the way to Baltimore, because I was terrified of what might be waiting there when we arrived.

Thanking God when we arrived everything was smooth sailing and no drama. We started packing and loading the truck so that we could get back on the road back to New York. Once we arrived I knew it was over and I was free, the hard part was over at least, it could only get easier from here. Back in New York things were placed in storage until I could find a place for me and my son, and that wouldn't be easy at all. But after 6 months of continuing to pave the pavement something finally came through.

Once getting settled into my new Bronx apartment, things started to come together, although I was a little nervous about moving to the same borough he was from in fear one day I would run into him. It was that moment I decided I wasn't going to live in fear anymore, that if I had seen him in the street I was prepared for whatever may happen to me. Because I knew that I had fought with everything I had to be free of such evilness. I had taken control of my life once again and was determined to fight for it till the bitter end. Before I knew it a year had gone by and not another word from the man who had made my life and my kids life a living hell.

In taking my life back I discovered my true self-worth. I now know what I will and will not except in relationships. If for any reason I feel uncomfortable, I express my feelings and let it be known. I refuse to except anything less of the expectations I have now set forth in place, that wasn't in place before. We never know how strong we are until we are faced with challenges. So I am proud to say that I am now a QUEEN who stood up, I now will know only expect to be treated like the queen I am. I now know the true meaning of self-love.

It's truly sad I had to endure the pain of two abusive relationships, in order to put the puzzle back together again whole. Although my spirit and soul was broken, today I still stand stronger, restored and DOMESTIC VIOLENCE FREE! For everyone who reads this I hope it helps to inspire and encourage you to know that you are not alone. Never give up faith, faith is what will carry you through the hard times, helping you to know this situation is temporary. The first step for me was to confront what I was experiencing.

I am proud to say it feels good to have taken my QUEENISM back. I vow that I will never allow myself to get lost in a man. That I now hold my worth close to my heart and will now only share myself with those that are worthy. We are all Queens, and we must know that it holds so much power. Domestic Violence has become this huge epidemic which is now beginning to plague our schools and younger generation. We must teach our kids their worth, this starts at home. In seeing my middle sister stay in and out of abusive relationships, I couldn't understand until I was faced with the same struggles as I became an adult.

My take away for my readers would be to know their never alone, there is always help to seek, you just have to take the first step towards wanting and knowing you deserve better. I am proud to say with all of Melissa's success up to this point after surviving two abusive relationships, I just finally realize I gained wealth which was priceless the minute I walked away and did not return; that was all the success I could have ever want or ask for. There is strength in numbers, and there is power in prayer.

15. THE AFTERMATH

So now here I am years later after surviving 2 consecutive abusive relationships, but I still suffer with the after affects. I thought once I learned how to forgive myself and learned how to manage coping skills intended to assist me with living in society having a 'normal', that things would get better and I could move forward with my life. I realize I needed help to get myself under control. I started feeling depressed and I was having panic attacks often. I was suffering with insomnia, and some days I really don't know to control what I was feeling. So I started to think counseling was an order. I did some research, and found someone. I called and made an appointment for intake, and was able to get an appointment right away. That was truly a blessing because I had become so deep in depression I started to feel suicidal.

After reaching this point of depression seeking therapy was actually the best decision I could of ever made for myself. I had become a ticking time bomb and I was ready to exploded any minute. After being accessed by intake and assigned a counselor, my healing began, but I still needed meds to help me get over the edge. After listening to what the counselor said to me about the possibilities of being on meds for the remainder of my life, I quickly knew what needed to be done. I decided I was not going to be on meds the rest of my life, medication kept me zoned out all the time. So I decided to do group counseling three times a week, and individual counseling two times a week. I did this same routine for 6 months.

After completing the very intense therapy, I finally felt like I was healthier and things had become much clearer. Although I was still on medication, I wasn't where I was 6 months prior when I was on 4 medications to keep me mellowed out. With all the hard work I began healing from the inside out. I did some deep soul searching, I was totally committed to the process, and as a result I discovered my purpose. I wanted to help other woman who were victims, or survivors understand that they weren't alone. I also understood that in order for me to help others, I myself had to get healthy, because an empty vessel cannot give.

With this new revelation I became more excited to challenge myself, to step outside of my comfort zone, to reinvent the new

Melissa who then could become the voice for the voiceless. With my healing came a new healthier, stronger, wiser and most importantly a SURVIVOR who became educated and more informative about domestic violence.

I realized I went from victim to victor because the hard part was now behind me. I had become a true fighter in every sense of the word, I fought to get of the anti-depressants. I went from being on 4 medications daily to 2 now and that's only for insomnia & anxiety.

 I fought to educate others I started to create my very own platforms, to stand in the front lines to tell my story to each and every person who would listen, and anyone who would give me a chance to tell my story. Speaking out against domestic violence became my life. I decided I was going to dedicate my life to helping other broken women. Broken women are totally misunderstood especially if you don't speak their language (meaning if you have never experienced dv). I wanted to make sure that people understood the mind of someone who has been abused, because our thinking process is confusing for the most part. The new Melissa was prepared to enlighten people about domestic violence.

Being in 2 abusive relationships made me the individual I am today, it has inspired me to inspire others with my story of cheating death twice. The victims aren't to blame, let's put the blame where it should be an that's with the abuser...

10 Most Common Signs of Domestic Violence and Abuse:

Some sign of domestic violence and abuse are more obvious than others; these are a few of the most common.

Does your partner ever....

1) Accuse you of cheating and being disloyal?

2) Make you feel worthless?

3) Hurt you by hitting, choking, or kicking you?

4) Intimidate and threatens to hurt you or someone you love?

5) Threatens to hurt themselves if they don't get what they want?

6) Try to control what you do and who you see?

7) Isolates you?

8) Pressure or force you into unwanted sex?

9) Controls your access to money

10) Stalks you, including calling you constantly or following you?

If you suspect that you are experiencing domestic violence or relationship abuse know:

> You have rights
> You can get help
> You are not alone
> You are NOT to blame
> You DO NOT deserve to be treated this way

Domestic Violence Hotline # 800-799-SAFE(7233)
or reach out to www.loveshouldnthurtny.com
or Melissaholmes67.mh@gmail.com

LOVE SHOULDN'T HURT NY

Love Shouldn't Hurt is a Domestic Violence Awareness and Support Group (LSH). LSH is comprised of victims, survivors and supporters. After surviving two abusive relationships, I Melissa Holmes, started LSH as a secret group on the social networking site Facebook. I was looking for an arena to vent, post and provide support for people who have also suffered abuse. LSH started with about 30 members, we now have well over 1000 members worldwide.

LSH is giving a sense of purpose through daily prayers and supportive post, motivating people to leave abusive situations, and helping victims heal after abuse. LSH has assisted victims escape from their abusers. For 4 years LSH has encouraged, enhanced, empowered and elevated Domestic Violence awareness. Now we are campaigning against Domestic Violence in communities by paying forward what we receive inside LSH with combined acts of service and support.

To learn more visit: www.loveshouldnthurtny.com

LOVE SHOULDN'T HURT

CPSIA information can be obtained
at www.ICGtesting.com
Printed in the USA
LVOW08s0380911   16

5122 1LV00007B/150/P